DOG

GROOMING

WITHOUT FEAR OR FORCE

Incorporating Tellington TTouch®
and Other Positive Techniques

DAWN HARKIN & GLYNIS STEWART

TABLE OF CONTENTS

FOREWORD

When I first met Glynis and Dawn at one of their early practitioner training courses, I sensed that, though keen and excited about the method, they were apprehensive about how much TTouch they could use in their grooming practice. After all, you have time constraints to keep up with, back-to-back appointments and an expectation from the clients about getting the job done.

Despite any apprehension about practical application, Dawn and Glynis "just did the work". Integrating what they learned from TTouch and other positive-based approaches, they discovered how much easier and low-stress the entire grooming experience could be with very little extra time. Thanks to their passion for making a groom a kinder and less stressful experience for animals, they were able to combine their skills in a positive way for everyone involved.

Their experience has resulted in a program for groomers, which they have spread throughout the UK. Now it also appears in this well-laid-out book. "Grooming Without Fear or Force" is concise, well-thought-out and thorough. The chapters are easy to follow, offer specific approaches to various grooming concerns and provide great examples of dogs that have overcome their fears.

This is a fabulous example of applied TTouch. I am very

proud to have been part of their process and so excited about what they are offering to groomers to make the experience safer and more positive for both two- and four-legged beings.

Robyn Hood – Senior Instructor of Tellington Touch®

INTRODUCTION

Our Journey

Our journey began back in 2009. We met during a dog grooming training course and have been best friends ever since. At the time, neither of us had a clue about grooming, handling dogs or, for that matter, how we or the dogs in our care might react in the grooming environment.

It has certainly been an eye-opener. One thing we have always been extremely passionate about is the welfare of the animal in our care and on our grooming table.

As professional dog groomers, we both felt the job was more than that. Too often, we were seeing and dealing with challenging situations in the grooming room. We wanted to be more than "good" professional dog groomers. Our goal was to improve our services not only by giving the best treatment possible in the grooming environment but also by helping the more nervous, anxious and reactive doggie clients that we frequently see.

And so, we decided to explore the benefits of Tellington TTouch®. After our first workshop and our introduction to Sarah Fisher, we were hooked! Seeing the impact that this amazing technique has on our companion animals, we decided to make these canines' grooming experiences more positive.

The TTouch journey began!

Training with Sarah Fisher and Robyn Hood at Tilly Farm was an amazing experience. The wealth of knowledge we received has given us skills that have transformed the way we groom and handle the dogs in our salons on a daily basis.

We are qualified Tellington TTouch® Practitioners with a number of grooming establishments and training academies under our belts. We have taught in our own academies, held workshops and seminars at major grooming events, and offered training days at centres and colleges across the country. We have a wealth of experience that we continue to share with the grooming world.

Too often we hear about difficult situations in the grooming environment. Every dog groomer has experienced some form of unwanted behaviour from our four-legged clients. These situations can seem a bit frustrating, as time is precious and the job needs to be done. So, what to do?

The magic of Tellington TTouch® has made a massive difference in our daily working lives. To be frank, we can't work without this amazing technique and some other interesting skills and practices we have picked up throughout our journey.

We are constantly seeking to enrich the grooming process for both groomers and our doggie clients:

- ✓ We run stand-alone TTouch courses and workshops at our academies and throughout the UK, hosted at individual grooming centres.
- ✓ We are the only two grooming academies in the UK that teach TTouch alongside professional grooming courses.

- ✓ We have developed a Level 3 TTouch accreditation with the Open College Network West Midlands (OCN). A TTouch grooming qualification is evolving as we speak.
- ✓ We continue to be invited by several colleges to host TTouch courses for dog groomers and canine professionals.
- ✓ We regularly speak at major grooming events by invitation, spreading the magic of TTouch for groomers.
- ✓ And now we have our book!!

If any of these courses or workshops are of interest to you, please contact us. Our details can be found at the back of the book.

In this book, we will show how the "magic" can work for you, too.

What is Tellington TTouch®?

Tellington TTouch® (TTouch) was developed in the equine world over 40 years ago by Linda Tellington Jones. It has since been developed further to include our companion animals and even us humans. It is now widely used around the world by trainers, shelter workers, veterinarians, dog groomers, physiotherapists, behaviour counsellors, veterinary nurses and dog owners, to mention a few.

It recognises an inextricable link between posture and behaviour and uses bodywork, groundwork exercises and specific equipment to release tension, improve posture and promote a feeling of calm and wellbeing.

TTouch engages the parasympathetic nervous system, which helps slow the heart and breathing rate, release muscle tension, lower the blood pressure, and improve circulation, balance and posture. This process helps the animal learn how to respond appropriately to situations rather than simply react.

The intent of TTouch is to activate the function of the cells and awaken cellular intelligence – a little like "turning on the electric lights of the body." By working on the nervous system, it sends a message to the body. The act of providing beneficial information via the nervous system helps a dog learn.

It is a respectful way of building a relationship with a dog or any other animal and it offers many benefits, including improving the physical, mental and emotional wellbeing of the dogs in our care.

Physical

Mental

Emotional

By reducing unwanted behaviours and helping dogs develop self-confidence and self-control, this system enables them to move beyond their instinctive – and often fearful – responses.

In the grooming environment, TTouch is a perfect method of working with dogs, without fear or force. It has helped with numerous challenges over the years and has changed the way we work every day.

Benefits of TTouch for Groomers

Most of the time we love our job, though every day we face numerous challenges in the grooming environment. But let's face it: We have a job to do. So, how can we, as groomers, make our lives easier while enriching the visit to our grooming spa for our four-legged friends? This is not an easy task when we are dealing with sometimes very demanding situations.

The following is not an exhaustive list by any means. However, it contains some of the everyday challenges to which you will be able to relate. TTouch – and some other practices we have learned – can be used to help alleviate some of our everyday pressures:

- ➤ Entering the grooming environment
- ➤ Bathing
- ➤ Drying
- ➤ Standing up/Posture
- ➤ Trimming nails/feet
- ➤ Trimming around the eyes
- ➤ Trimming around the rear end or tail
- ➤ Handling
- ➤ Noise sensitivity
- ➤ Touch sensitive
- ➤ Excitability
- ➤ Fear
- ➤ Anxiety

"JUST ANOTHER DAY AT THE OFFICE"

The techniques we use are based on co-operation and respect. Using a combination of specific touches lifts, and movement exercises helps release tension and increase body awareness, allowing dogs to be handled without provoking typical fear responses.

You may ask: "What are the benefits of taking a few moments to apply TTouch in the grooming environment?" Here are a few outcomes we witness on a daily basis:

- ✓ Reduces stress, for both the groomer and the dog
- ✓ Improves balance
- ✓ Influences and changes behaviour
- ✓ Changes posture
- ✓ Releases tension
- ✓ Builds a better relationship between the handler and the dog
- ✓ Develops trust and understanding
- ✓ Changes the dog's expectation of what human contact means
- ✓ Influences the nervous system, activating cells (like switching on electric lights in the body)

When we use TTouch and a variety of other tools and techniques, we can help our four-legged friends experience self-confidence in previously frightening situations. The dogs in our care can then more easily learn new and more appropriate behaviours. Often, even the most difficult problems are eliminated.

Enriching the dog's experience in the grooming environment leads to a more positive experience for everyone concerned, and it doesn't have to take a long time to learn or apply.

HAPPY DOG = HAPPY OWNER
= HAPPY GROOMER

WIN-WIN!

Components

This book covers several TTouch components and other useful techniques

1	**Observations**
2	**Approach and Handling**
3	**Handling Assessment**
4	**Equipment**
5	**Bodywork**
6	**Groundwork**
7	**Handler Posture**

How do we take the jigsaw pieces and apply them to the grooming process? This book provides lots of information and will guide you through some simple steps to improving the grooming process and enriching the environment for both dog and groomer.

This book details components 1-5, to help with everyday grooming situations.

It is not necessary to understand the dog's anatomy or to have specialised knowledge. Anyone can apply the techniques; with practice, they will become second nature.

Groundwork – an important element of TTouch work – is not covered in this edition for grooming. Groundwork is a series of slow, on-lead exercises to improve balance, co-ordination and posture. It is a playground for higher learning.

In the context of grooming, "handler posture" generally means that whatever you, as a groomer, are feeling while handling a dog will transfer down to the piece of equipment being used (for example, scissors, comb, sponge). Always try to be positive and calm, which, as we know, can sometime be a challenge.

Observations

Before we begin any part of the grooming process, it is important that we take time to observe and assess the dog in our care. When we piece together information, a picture will emerge that will help improve the grooming process for both dog and handler. Win-win all around!

As we have the dog in our care for at least two hours, we have an opportunity to see how the dog responds to the grooming environment and to the handling which goes along with it. We can't know what is going on inside a dog's mind; we must look at, listen to and feel what is going on with the dog in our care so that we can adjust our handling accordingly.

This is not an exhaustive list, but some things to consider when assessing a dog in the grooming environment are:

Behaviour & responses to stimuli and mood
Freezing

Barking

Trembling

Vocalizing

Pay attention to the sound a dog makes. Excessive panting, whining or barking could indicate stress.

Body language

Ear position/movement

Lip licking

Tail position/movement

Eyes glazed, staring, soft

Observe and notice changes in body language; this gives you the opportunity to pause and adjust the handling accordingly.

Posture & movement

Head position

Standing straight

Sitting position

Gait

Feet position

By watching the way a dog moves and responds in the grooming environment, you can gain insight into how the dog is feeling physically. You can also get invaluable information about the dog's mental and emotional states.

There is a pattern to both posture and behaviour. For example, dogs that are noise-sensitive tend to carry tension through their hindquarters. As the body releases tension, unwanted behaviours diminish.

Change the posture, change the behaviour! A dog's posture is affected by its emotions. If a dog is afraid, it may tuck its tail between its legs. If we can change the posture, we can change the behaviour.

Tension patterns & quality of coat

Coat patterns

Swirls

Hot/cold spots

Dandruff

Thinning, dense

Lay of the coat

The coat can provide lots of information. Look for hair that may be greasy or standing up, particularly around the back, neck or hindquarters. This may be an indication of tension in that part of the body. Dogs with coat changes may be more sensitive to touch in those areas.

Posture During Stress

During a stressful situation, adrenalin and cortisol hormones prepare the body for a fight-or-flight response. TTouch can help a dog recover more quickly, which is very helpful in the grooming environment

Some signs that dogs may display to indicate stress:

Body posture: arched back, hips down, rolling onto back, very still

Head carriage: Too high or too low

Breathing: Excessive panting, holding breath, sighing

Tail: Excessive wagging, tucked between legs, stiff

Mouth: Drooling, lips pulled back, puffed-up cheeks, dry, panting

Eyes: Whale eye (showing whites of eyes), wide open, squinting

Ears: Pulled back, erect

Learning to observe will enable you to make appropriate changes when handling a dog in your care. It will also help you decide which TTouches to use and where to use them.

REMEMBER:

OBSERVATIONS ARE AT THAT MOMENT IN TIME.

FOCUS on what you **SEE** rather than on what you believe might be happening.

Behaviour Triggers

Triggers =

One candle on its own may not seem to be a huge concern.

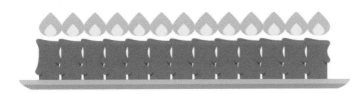

The more candles there are, the more volatile the situation.

Grooming

In grooming, let's imagine the dog in our care as a bank account and consider the dog grooming process to be a series of deposits and withdrawals. When we take a withdrawal (for example, trimming nails or plucking ears), we want to add a deposit (for example, TTouches, an enriched grooming environment and positive techniques). This way, when the dog

21

leaves the grooming salon, it isn't doing so with an emotional overdraft.

This is not an exhaustive list; some of these stimuli may trigger reactions:

Environment & Surroundings

Grooming Process

Equipment

Noise Sensitivity

Containment

Contact

Forceful Handling

Too many lit candles will eventually cause an eruption. By doing some TTouch bodywork, using body wraps and giving the dog a time out, we will help blow out the candles, or add deposits to the emotional "bank account".

Body Wraps

Body wraps are integral pieces of the Tellington TTouch® Method and are used to complement the bodywork.

When an animal holds its breath in fear, it goes into the instinctive mode of fight-or-flight. A dog that is anxious or fearful can go into freeze, become aggressive, lick compulsively, etc. The body wrap acts as a form of comforting contact, increasing the dog's body awareness. If used correctly, it can eliminate many issues a dog may experience during the grooming process.

Think of the body wrap in light of the concept of giving a 'security hug'.

When would we use a body wrap in the grooming salon?

➢ Fearful of nail clipping/clearing pads
➢ Hyperexcitability
➢ Separation anxiety
➢ Shyness, nervousness
➢ Waiting in holding area
➢ Dogs with arthritis
➢ Trembling, regardless of cause
➢ Helping to build confidence
➢ Bringing more awareness into the body
➢ Preparing for the use of a restraint on a grooming table or in the bath

- ➢ Car sickness (advise the owner)
- ➢ Vocal dogs
- ➢ Pre-clipping the coat with a body wrap on

The wraps are different widths (1-4 inch) of a stretchy elastic bandage (Ace brand). They should never be put on too tightly. Make sure the wraps are snug enough to stay on but are not overstretched.

Observe the dog's posture, respiration and reactions. If the dog seems overwhelmed, goes into freeze or tries to remove the wrap, take it off immediately and maybe try it again later or alter the configuration.

Always observe and let the dog be the judge. Pay close attention to responses and act accordingly.

Quarter wrap

This is probably the easiest and most common wrap we use in the grooming salon. It's the easiest option for the dog to accept and it has a nice introductory configuration. It is easy to apply, so we have found this wrap to be a good choice for more reactive, anxious dogs that struggle to keep still.

What you need

2", 3" or 4" wrap depending on the dog's size

How to apply

Introduce the dog gently to the wrap. Let the dog smell the wrap. Gently place the wrap over the back. Position it about 1/3 of the way from the end, in the middle of the dog's upper chest. Keep the short end over the centre of the back. Gently bring up the ends on either side to cross over the shoulders. Cross the wrap over and bring the longer end under the dog's stomach. Fasten the wrap on the dog's side, either by tying it or by using a safety pin. Avoid tying the wrap right on the spine so as not to put pressure on that area.

See steps 1 – 7.

Half wrap

The half wrap is another popular wrap. It helps bring awareness to the front and middle parts of the dog. It is easy to apply and can help a dog adjust to the challenging situations it will face during the grooming process. Many shy or nervous dogs find this configuration easy to accept.

How to apply

Introduce to the dog to the half wrap the same way you would with the quarter wrap (steps 1-6). Place the wrap again around and under the dog's stomach (step 8). Bring the remainder of the wrap up to one side and fasten the ends. Avoid tying the wrap right on the spine so as not to put pressure on that area.

Step 1 – Let the dog smell the wrap to get accustomed to it.

Step 2 – Place the wrap over the back of the dog for initial contact.

Step 3 – Place the wrap over the front of the dog for position 1 of the quarter wrap.

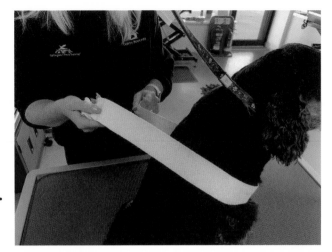

Step 4 – Gently bring up the ends on either side (position 2).

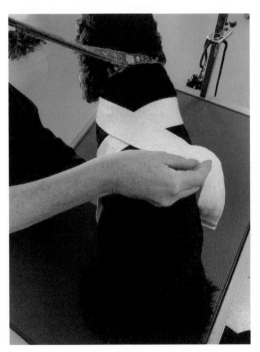

Step 5 – Cross over the shoulders (position 3).

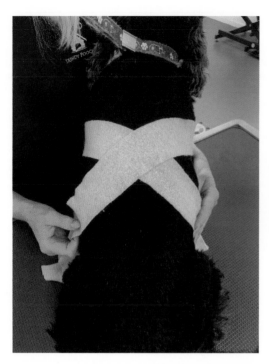

Step 6 – Cross the wrap over the shoulders and bring the longer end under the dog's stomach (position 4).

Step 7 – Fasten the wrap on the dog's side by either tying it or using a safety pin.

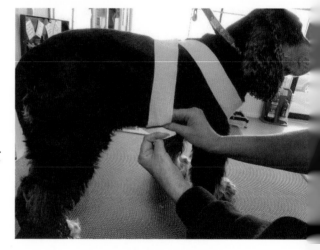

Quarter wrap

Step 8 – Follow steps 1-6, then continue and place the wrap again around and under the dog's stomach. Fasten the wrap on the dog's side by either tying it or using a safety pin.

Half wrap

Head wrap

Head wraps create a thinking cap and help the dog focus and calm down. Always read the dog carefully; if the dog shows signs of being uncomfortable with the wrap or tries to remove the wrap, change what you are doing or remove the wrap completely.

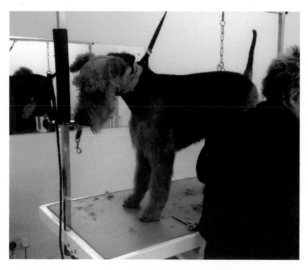

An example of a head wrap in use when grooming

Face wrap

You can use a 1" or 2" wrap, or sewing elastic on smaller dogs.

This configuration sits over the muzzle and then around the back of the head, gently cradling the jowl.

We would use this type of head wrap on a dog that was barking or whining, or on a reactive dog.

How to apply

Begin by putting the middle of the bandage across the nose. Cross the ends under the chin. Take the ends behind the head and fasten with a light knot, Velcro or a safety pin.

Some dogs may find that wearing a hair scrunchie placed over the nose is more acceptable. This is also easier to apply.

Neck wrap

Use a 1" or 2" wrap.

This configuration winds loosely around the dog's neck.

It can be used to help a head-shy dog accept the restraint on the grooming table or in the bath. This wrap can also change a high-headed dog's posture, giving the dog more confidence and helping the dog relax.

How to apply

Gently wind the wrap 2½ to 3 times around the dog's neck. Fasten loosely. Remove immediately if the dog shows signs of discomfort.

Thundershirts

Thundershirts can also help dogs in the grooming environment. They provide benefits similar to those of body wraps. They look more attractive, but they also come at an added expense.

Thundershirts can help dogs with nervousness, separation anxiety, travelling or hyperactivity. They can alleviate noise phobia and help dogs cope during their time in the crate or holding area.

The material stretches and places gentle pressure over the body. This "swaddling" can help relax and ground the dog.

The Thundershirt is fastened with Velcro, which can be noisy during removal. This may startle dogs that are more nervous.

T-Shirts

As an alternative, T-shirts can be used for smaller dogs who seem to prefer softer material that isn't fastened by Velcro. However, depending on the style of T-shirt, it can be difficult to put on the dog, especially dogs that are head shy.

TTouch Bodywork

TTouch bodywork is vital for groomers – and the dogs in our care – during the challenges we face every day.

To support handling and reduce built-up tension in an already stressful situation, as well as to improve and build trust and a connection with the dogs in the grooming environment, one of the three categories of TTouch can be applied:

The bodywork TTouches:

➢ Circles
➢ Slides
➢ Lifts

The TTouch bodywork is a method of applying non-threatening contact which can increase levels of the hormone oxytocin. This will help override the fight-or-flight responses. It can be applied to any part of the dog's body; you don't need to know the anatomy.

The "rule" is to read the dog. If at any point the dog becomes uncomfortable or moves away, stop and give the dog a moment. At no point should you force the dog to accept being touched.

The TTouch bodywork will help increase circulation and awareness, boost the immune system, release tension and create a sense of calm in the grooming environment. This is important for both the dog and the groomer.

Learning a few TTouches can make a huge difference to you and the dog in your care. Remember to stay relaxed and breathe when doing the TTouch bodywork so that you don't affect the touches being applied. Be mindful to pause, giving the dog time to process the information. This mindful contact can change behaviour by influencing the nervous system.

The Basic Circular Method

Step 1: Imagine the face of a clock on your skin, approximately 1cm (1/2 inch).

Step 2: With a soft, straight wrist, place all your fingers together anywhere that the dog accepts. Keep your thumb lightly anchored against the dog's body to steady your hand.

Step 3: Begin at 6 o'clock, then move the skin clockwise around the circle, finishing at 9 o'clock. This creates a one-and-a-quarter circle.

The hand moves the surface of the skin, not the muscle. DO NOT slide over the skin or apply too much pressure, turning it into a massage.

Normally, a clockwise direction is applied but this can be altered to anti-clockwise if doing so is more comfortable for you and the dog.

Pressure of Touch

TTouch pressure is measured on a scale of 1-10. The most popular for dogs is 1-4. Start with number 1 pressure, which is the lightest. See how the dog reacts. Too light may be "tickly" while too much will turn into a massage.

It's important to find the scale of pressure and speed of movement that feel "right" to both groomer and dog. Keep it gentle, mindful and slow!

When you apply TTouch bodywork, the dog can be in any position that is comfortable for it. Make sure your own position is also relaxed so that you do not affect the application of the TTouches.

Abalone TTouch

Lightly place the flat of your hand on the dog's body. Your whole hand must move the skin in a one-and-a-quarter circle.

With the other hand, support the body. This will establish a connection. Pause after three or four TTouches to give the nervous system time to integrate the TTouches.

This TTouch is ideal for sensitive dogs due to the contact of the whole hand, which provides warmth and security. It also helps relax and calm down a nervous dog. Use number 1 or 2 pressure.

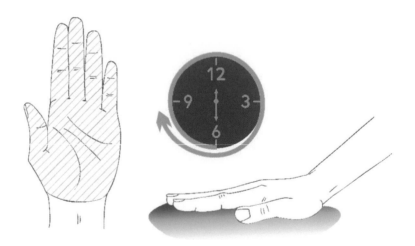

Lying Leopard TTouch

The area of contact used for this touch is the fingers.

Placing your hand lightly on the dog's body, use the underside of your fingers to gently move the skin in a basic one-and-a-quarter circle.

With this TTouch, you can use both your fingers and the palm of your hand. However, on smaller areas (such as the head or a leg), you wouldn't use the palm of your hand.

This TTouch is useful for nervous or hyperactive dogs.

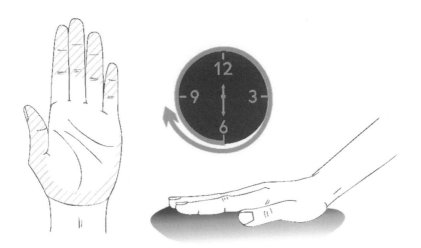

Clouded Leopard TTouch

Make sure your thumb remains anchored on the dog's body.

Clouded Leopard is the foundation of all the circular TTouches. It can be done all over the dog.

This TTouch is very effective for nervous and anxious dogs. It can help dogs feel confident in new and challenging situations.

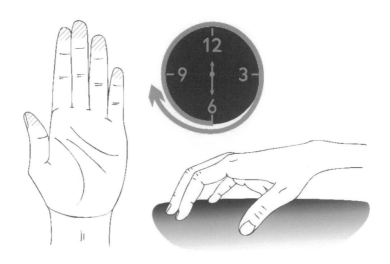

Raccoon TTouch

Curve your fingers and, using their very tips, apply tiny, one-and-a-quarter circles. Keep your hand and fingers soft, allowing movement through the knuckles.

Use light pressure – number 1 or 2.

Raccoon is the smallest of the TTouches and is applied mainly on smaller body parts such as the toes, the base of the ear and the back of the skull.

It is often used on smaller breeds and puppies. This TTouch promotes healing and can reduce pain or sensitive areas. It also reduces swelling and improves circulation.

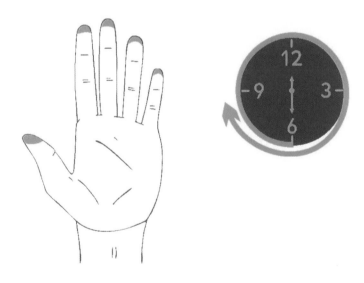

The Chimp TTouch

Bend your fingers towards the palm of your hand. Then, using the flat part between the first and second finger joints of the back of your hand, apply a one-and-a-quarter circle.

If you are working on a small dog or puppy, adjust the TTouch and use the back of the fingers up to the first joint. This is called Baby Chimp TTouch; the connection to the animal is softer.

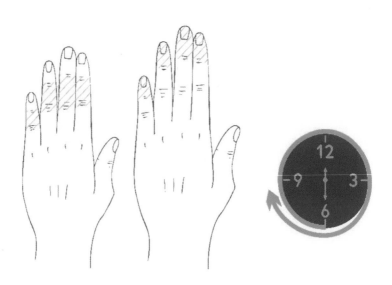

Llama TTouch

This TTouch involves using the back of the hand or the fingers to make a one-and-a-quarter circle starting at 6 o'clock. Make sure the pressure is light; you can apply it with the entire hand or just the knuckles. You can also use the side of your hand.

The Llama TTouch can be used on dogs that are afraid of an open hand coming towards them, as if to grab them. When you use the back of your hand, the approach is less threatening.

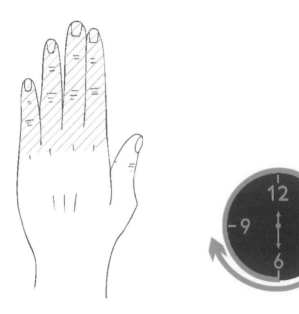

Noah's March

You can use Noah's March as an introduction as well as a finishing a session, with the back or palm of your hand.

Place your hand lightly on the dog's body and make smooth, sliding contact from the head, across the back and down the hindquarters.

This can be done whilst the dog is lying down or in a standing position.

Do this mindfully with your fingers slightly spread. For this TTouch, most dogs prefer light contact.

Noah's March is a sliding TTouch used to finish a session. The gentle, sliding strokes connect the entire body and combine the circular TTouches.

Ear TTouch

Ear work is a lovely way to connect with the dog. It is particularly effective at calming excited or hyperactive dogs. It has been used to prevent or reduce shock after injury.

Step 1

Starting at the top of the ear, do one ear at a time.

Step 2

Gently slide down the ear.

Continue sliding down the ear till you get to the tip. In some cases, with cocker spaniels' ears being quite heavy, you may want to finish the ear slide to the side of the ear.

Step 3

Step 4

Finish the slides using the back of your hand. This is called Noah's March. It is one of the sliding TTouches that we often use to end a TTouch session.

Upright Ears

Dogs with upright ears, such as German Shepherds, French bulldogs, etc., are sometimes more sensitive to ear slides. If they show signs of discomfort, try using your fingertips to do small, circular TTouches around the base or edges of the ear. This is called Raccoon TTouch.

DO NOT DO EAR TOUCHES ON DOGS WITH A HEART CONDITION!

Zebra TTouch

Zebra helps release tension and connects the different parts of the body. This TTouch can be used to initiate contact and help assess areas on the dog's body that may be sensitive to contact.

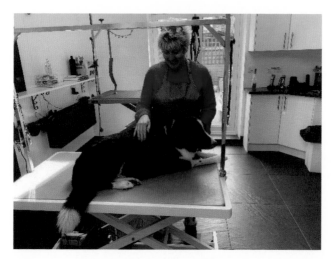

Step 1

Start with your fingers together on an area that the dog is comfortable with.

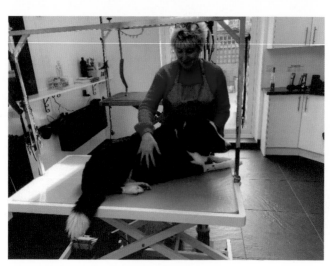

Step 2

Slowly spread apart your fingers and move in a diagonal line across the body.

Step 3
Continue sliding zig-zag movements along the dog's body.

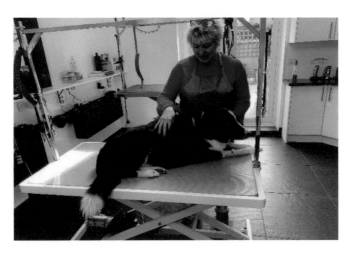

Be mindful to keep your wrists straight and your fingers spread and relaxed.

The movement should be done rhythmically. At all times, make sure the dog is coping with the placement of your hands.

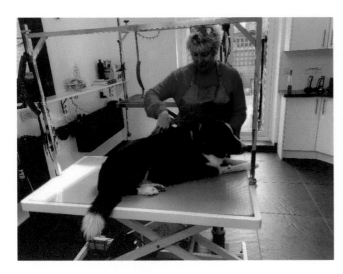

Step 4

Remember to pause when moving over the dog's body

Python TTouch

Front Legs

Starting at the side of the dog, place your hand around the leg, just below the elbow. For large dogs, use both hands. For small dogs, use just your fingers.

Take in a breath before starting. Then slowly exhale as you gently lift the skin and muscle. Without changing your contact or pressure, slowly return the skin to the start, inhaling as you do this. Then slide down about one-half inch after each lift until you reach the paws.

Upper Part of the Hind Legs

Encircle the thigh with the flat of your hands, placing your thumbs on the outside of the thigh or placing one hand on the inside and one hand on the outside.

Lower Part of the Hind Legs

Because the lower part of the hind legs is much smaller, you can encircle it with both hands or use just one hand. When you have reached the paws, do Noah's March on the entire leg from top to bottom.

Python TTouches can be performed anywhere on the body. They promote calmness and relaxation with dogs that are shy, tense or hyperactive. These TTouches can help the dog become more grounded, which promotes mental, emotional and physical balance.

Jelly Fish

Gently place your fingertips or hand on the dog's body. Make mindful "jiggling" movements, similar to a vibration, on the area where you are about to start clipping or washing. This is a nice way to introduce the clippers.

In terms of whether to use the whole hand, the palm or the fingers, apply whichever feels most comfortable for both you and the dog.

Hair Slides

Take some hair between your thumb and index finger. Gently slide up from the root and move in the direction of the hair. Go to the tips of the hair. If the dog's hair is too short to do hair slides, you can gently lift the skin with your thumb and index finger and slide along the hair slowly, letting go of the skin avoid pinching the dog.

Hair slides can be an enjoyable introduction to TTouch bodywork, as they help the dog relax. They are particularly effective with dogs that are fearful of grooming and with vocal dogs.

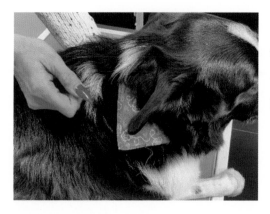

This is a lovely TTouch to use on long-haired breeds.

Mouth Work

This helps overly sensitive and vocal dogs relax and become more focussed. Before beginning any mouth work, you should check the dog's teeth and gums to make sure there is no inflammation which may cause discomfort or pain.

With soft hands, begin around the neck and head area, using the Lying Leopard or Chimp TTouches. Gradually move to the muzzle. If safe to do so, you can then gently slide your finger under the lips and use Raccoon TTouches on the gums.

Air Circles

Make the movement of a circle whilst using a brush, the wand or a feather, above the area you want to influence, without touching the dog.

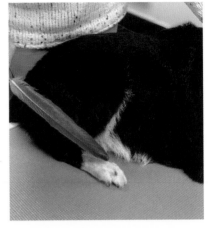

For example: Make air circles above the toes and feet before attempting nail clipping.

Tail Work

This helps reduce tension in the back and hindquarters. It is also good for dogs that fear loud noises.

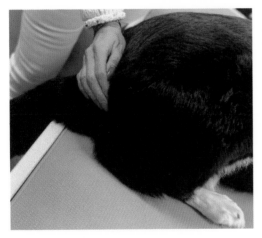

Start by cupping your hand over the base of the tail and apply one-and-a-quarter circles. Continue with Raccoon TTouches or Hair Slides along the entire tail.

Circling the tail at the base can also help release tension.

"Quiet the tail, quiet the dog."

Approach and Handling

It is important to be able to handle a dog in the grooming environment without upsetting either the dog or the groomer. This process starts right at the beginning, when the dog enters the grooming salon. Try to adopt a "first date" approach.

Before approaching or greeting the dog, give it a moment while you engage with the owner, all the while observing movement, posture and behaviours.

Look at how the dog gathers data from the environment as you also start gathering data from the dog and its owner. Look for behaviours, signs of stress and reactions to the environment. Then adopt appropriate actions.

Examples might be:

➢ Problems walking on certain floor coverings
➢ Posture
➢ Fear of other dogs, sounds or new environments
➢ Cowering, panting
➢ Tail lowered or wagging excessively
➢ Wary of approach
➢ Etc.

If you approach the dog correctly, you should minimise unwanted reactions and the risk of injury. You will also help improve relations and establish a better connection with the dog.

Dogs may engage in displacement activities (such as fidgeting, sniffing, fooling around, etc.) if they are struggling with a situation or are unable to move away from something that concerns them. Therefore, getting the approach and handling correct for dog groomers is a must.

HOW NOT TO APPROACH:

DON'T lean over, stand in front of or crowd the dog.

Standing in front of the dog and giving too much eye contact can be seen as threatening and can put you at risk of being bitten.

Always give the dog the chance to move away from you.

CORRECT WAY TO APPROACH:

When first approaching the dog, start from the side. Watch the dog's responses and look carefully at the body language.

Treat the encounter as a "first date" and give the dog a choice.

Use the back of your hand to initiate contact. Avoid leaning over the dog and invading its space.

Gently glide the back of your hand along the side of the dog's body. This will appear less grabby and threatening.

Observe the dog's behaviour, movement and posture for indications on how the dog might be feeling about your approach. Move closer to the dog only when it's appropriate to do so.

Many dogs are sensitive to contact on the back. Dogs that are wary about contact on the back and spine may have soft tissue injuries or skeletal problems.

With the back of your hand, check the dog for temperature changes, i.e. hot or cold spots or sensitive areas. This will give you information for handling your four-legged visitor in the bath or on the grooming table.

Once the owner hands the lead over to you, moving the dog into the grooming room or bathroom can sometimes prove challenging in itself.

If the dog freezes or doesn't want to move, gently stroking the lead can encourage movement.

When you stroke a loose lead, you gently give signals to the dog to move without forcing the dog to do so. Try not to pull the lead; give the dog a moment if needed.

Step 1

Make sure the lead is loose; don't pull on it. Stand parallel to the dog's shoulders and make sure there is enough of a gap between you so that dog can move or turn.

Step 2

Start with the hand farthest away from you and stroke the lead towards you gently and slowly with alternate hands by moving one hand over the top of the other. Continue with even contact on the lead until the dog moves and looks at where you want to go.

Step 3

Keep stroking the lead and ask the dog to move forward.

Don't rush or pull the lead if the dog doesn't respond straight away. Pause and give the dog a moment.

Step 4

Make sure you aren't tense through your own body while stroking the lead evenly and gently maintaining contact on the lead. Keep moving forward, encouraging the dog.

Contain Versus Restrain

What do we mean by "Contain Vs Restrain" and how can this knowledge help us in the grooming environment?

Every day, groomers face challenges with things like:

➢ Dogs reacting when they are handled on the grooming table or in the bath
➢ Cutting nails and holding legs/feet
➢ Difficulty in picking up dogs
➢ Overhandling
➢ Correct use of restraints on the grooming table or in the bath

Equally, every day, dogs face challenges in the grooming environment:

➢ Forceful handling that causes panic
➢ Fear of the unknown, leading to anxiety
➢ Panic when approached or picked up
➢ Sensitivity to being handled
➢ Lack of choices

There is a huge difference between the two. Containing means asking for permission and is a far more respectful approach. Restraining is forceful; it causes resistance and can lead to panic or a struggle – and, quite possibly, a fight-or-flight reaction.

How many of us do not want others to enter our personal space? Forced contact with someone isn't a very nice prospect, so why should the dogs in our care in a grooming environment accept this kind of approach? As groomers, we must remember that we are temporary guardians of these dogs and that it is not appropriate for us to force any kind of overhandling or restraint on them while they are in our care.

"Contain" rather than restrain is the key. If you cannot touch a dog at all, it makes sense that trying to pick up that dog to put it on a grooming table or in a bath could end in disaster.

So, how do we contain?

By holding the dog in a non-threating manner: Arms, shoulders and hands relaxed, moving with the dog as opposed to stopping the movement. This way, the dog has freedom of choice to move around while you remain connected in a safe way. Pulling at a dog will only cause an opposition reflex, with the dog pulling away and starting a "tug of war".

Containing will encourage trust and confidence between handler and dog. Through the use of TTouch and a variety of other tools and techniques, containment becomes much easier to achieve

Nellie is turning away, displaying a clear calming signal because she feels overwhelmed by being RESTRAINED.

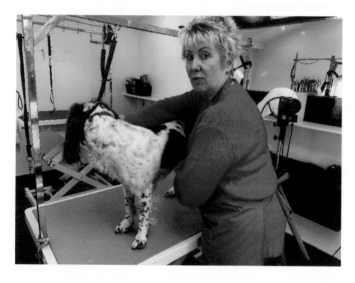

Here, she is CONTAINED. A change in our approach can help a dog feel relaxed and secure on the grooming table.

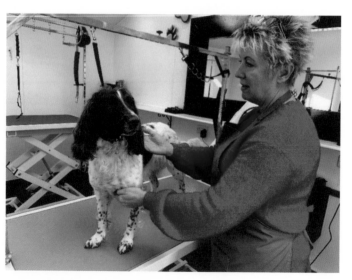

Tool Kit

TTouch works on the nervous system, helping to improve mental, physical and emotional balance. It creates an enhanced ability to learn and co-operate by opening new channels of communication. One of the most exciting things about this work is that it constantly evolves as we experiment and add tools to our toolbox.

Below are some of the different types of equipment we use for TTouch in the grooming environment.

- ✓ Body wraps
- ✓ Thundershirts
- ✓ T-shirts
- ✓ Palm and bath mitts
- ✓ Sponges
- ✓ Hoodies
- ✓ Calming bands
- ✓ Brushes
- ✓ Hair scrunchies
- ✓ Feathers
- ✓ Wands
- ✓ Lick mats
- ✓ Snuffle mats

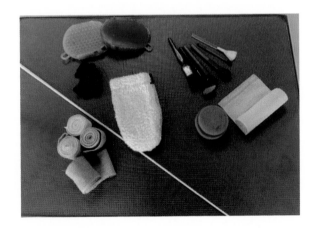

Use your imagination when thinking of equipment to use for grooming and TTouch.

GET CREATIVE!

With dogs that are nervous about direct hand contact, we use palm and bath mitts, or sponges.

With more reactive dogs, we use wands, (i.e. long dressage schooling sticks) to gently stroke the dog. This can be a safe starting point before we go in with our hands. Remember,

non-threatening contact can override the fight-or-flight response.

Happy Hoodies help the dog feel secure whilst it is being dried; they block out the noise of the dryer.

They can also stop a vocal dog from barking.

The use of a makeup brush or paintbrush around the eye area before trimming a dog's eyes with scissors helps the dog accept being handled around this area.

Gently stroke the area until the dog accepts you working closely around the eyes. Do this before introducing scissors.

Gently placing a hair scrunchy over the muzzle can help calm a vocal dog.

For dogs sensitive to touch around the face, use a bath scrunchy in a circular motion.

Calming Signals and Communication

WHAT are they?

AND what's the benefit of knowing about them for grooming?

Turid Rugaas has described many behaviours that dogs use to convey information to other animals and humans. She terms these "calming signals, the language of peace which enables dogs to avoid and solve conflicts".

It is vitally important that groomers recognize calming signals and be aware that these communication signs can progress to higher levels of stress, particularly if the signal is ignored or if the dog feels continually threatened. Some signs are very subtle

Some of the more obvious calming signals you may observe during the grooming process are:

- ➢ Barking
- ➢ Whining
- ➢ Growling
- ➢ Backing away
- ➢ Showing teeth
- ➢ Play bowing
- ➢ Etc.

Subtle signs that a dog may display before escalating into the more obvious signals might be:

- ➢ Dilated pupils
- ➢ Tightness around the eyes
- ➢ Whale eye/Half-moon eye
- ➢ Teeth chattering
- ➢ Cheek puffing
- ➢ Wrinkled muzzle
- ➢ Sitting down and lifting a paw
- ➢ Scratching
- ➢ Yawning
- ➢ Excess salivation
- ➢ Lip/Nose licking
- ➢ Panting
- ➢ Turning around/away
- ➢ Etc.

When we recognise these signs in the context of a grooming situation, we can change what we are doing and give the dog a moment.

Incorporating some TTouch bodywork into the grooming process allows us to build trust and confidence with the dog in our care. We can signal to the dog that we are "listening" to its concerns.

For example, if the dog starts to lip lick when you are trimming between the eyes, pause for a moment and do some gentle TTouch bodywork. This will release tension and help instil cooperation, building confidence.

During stressful situations such as grooming, adrenalin and cortisol prepare the dog for fight or flight. By using TTouch techniques and the available tool kit, we groomers can help reduce the stages of a stress-inducing situation.

REMEMBER, careful observation is the key to understanding what signals the dog in our care is trying to give us AND it is only at that moment in time. It is important to respond appropriately to avoid any escalation that may cause stress levels to rise and a confrontation to occur.

Coat Changes

Dog groomers see many different breeds and coat types. Very early in our training, we learn all about these coat types – for example, wool, wire, smooth, double, combination, etc.

What other considerations should we be noting? And why? We must consider the things we see every day, as this provides underlying information that we can use when handling the dogs in our care.

The coat and skin combined are the largest sensory organs and the outer layer of the skin forms the largest piece of connective tissue. Any changes in the soft tissue and skeleton will affect the texture and appearance of the coat as well as the mobility and temperature of the skin.

Some examples of coat changes for groomers to consider:

➢ Colour – light and dark
➢ Coarse, rough, dry or greasy hair
➢ Dandruff
➢ Bald patches
➢ Swirls and curls
➢ Areas that are slow to shed
➢ Etc.

Why is it important for dog groomers to be aware of coat changes?

By looking closer at the dog's coat, we can gather information:

> How and where does the hair stand up? If it is around the neck or hindquarters, it could indicate tension, with the tightness of the skin causing the hair to stand up.

> Is the coat greasy? If so, in what area? This could indicate that the dog is suffering from arthritis in that area.

> Dandruff or scurf could be due to tight skin or tension throughout the body.

> Swirls may be part of the dog's natural coat; however, they may also be caused by trauma such as an accident or they could appear after surgery.

> Colour changes, i.e. darkening or discoloured areas. Consider the possibility of an underlying health issue, as the coat is usually the first thing to change.

> Etc.

There are many examples to consider, so what do we do with this information once we have it?

Let's consider a greasy coat and a dog suffering from arthritis. This dog might struggle with being groomed due to pain, especially during the winter months. If we are aware of this condition, we can be more mindful in our handling and adapt the way we groom the dog. A small adjustment (such as using a calming cradle for clearing out pads) can make a huge difference for the dog.

As groomers, we are in a very fortunate position to notice coat changes. Upon taking in that information with our eyes, we can adjust our handling or change what we are doing.

Some coat change examples

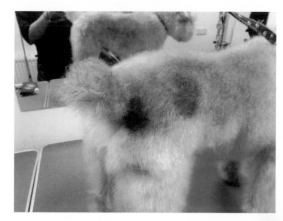

Skin condition after flea infestation

Arthritis in the back

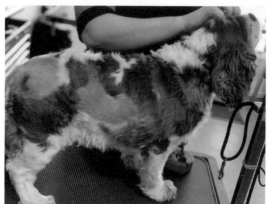

Noise sensitive

FREE WORK

The nature of free work gives a dog the opportunity to make a choice to engage or disengage. Letting the dog decide when it is ready to re-engage with us will help build relationships and stop the dog from becoming overwhelmed. This is important in the grooming environment, which can be a stress-inducing situation.

During the grooming process, the dog will sometimes struggle to cope with certain aspects of the groom. It may be fearful of the dryer or clippers. By letting the dog take a break and by introducing it to some free work, we will give the dog the opportunity to reset, rebalance and release any built-up tension.

Free work allows us to observe, highlighting subtle postural habits and concerns. It enables us to modify how and what we teach the dog and to see how the dog organises its body.

How Do We Set Up Free Work in the Grooming Environment?

First, it is important that we check with the owner to see if the dog has any dietary sensitivities or behaviour concerns around food.

Then we need to set up the environment with different surfaces/scent activities such as lick mats, snuffle mats or carpet/vinyl matting (get creative).

Place different treats in and around the area, making sure that you put some outside the area in case the dog struggles with certain textures.

Then let the dog choose which, if any, surfaces/treats it wants to engage with. All the while, observe the dog's actions and reactions.

GIVING THE DOG A MOMENT away from something it finds stressful can often save time in the long run.

Bucket Game

The Bucket Game, otherwise known as:

THE GAME OF CHOICE

This fun and easy training game is designed to empower the learners by creating an environment where the dogs have a choice and can communicate their intentions to participate.

The Bucket Game gives animals the ability to tell us:

- ➢ When they are comfortable and ready to start
- ➢ When they need to take a break
- ➢ When they want to stop
- ➢ Whether we need to slow down or change what we are doing

The Bucket Game was designed by Chirag Patel, a training

and behaviour expert. Chirag encourages conversations between animals and people. This game was initially designed to teach essential husbandry behaviours (i.e. those behaviours that allow your dog to actively participate in its daily and veterinary care).

This game can be integrated into your everyday grooming to help with things like nail trimming, ear plucking, etc. The process increases confidence and enhances the overall relationship between you and the dog in your care.

The Bucket Game uses shaping, targeting, stationing and many other behavioural principles in a way that makes it fun for both the animal and the caregiver.

What you will need:

- ➢ A bucket
- ➢ High-value treat or toy
- ➢ A bed/mat or safe place
- ➢ Water

1. The foundation of the game

Start by putting the rewards in the bucket and holding the bucket out to the side.

Reward the dog for looking at the bucket but keeping some distance from it (20-50cm). Reward the dog using treats from the bucket.

You can then put the bucket on the grooming table or a nearby shelf. Reward the dog for looking at it but not jumping or lunging towards it.

The position of the dog (e.g. sitting, lying down or standing) doesn't matter. The aim is to reward the dog for engaging with the bucket.

Start reinforcing when the dog maintains eye contact with the bucket for longer periods of time. Don't expand your criteria too soon or too quickly, as this may confuse the dog. The dog should be allowed to look around between periods of focusing on the bucket.

REMEMBER, this is a game of choice and a conversation between you and the dog. You do not need to call the dog, shake the bucket, tug on the restraint, etc. Let the dog decide whether to engage or participate in the training program.

2. Decide what you want to get the dog to let you do

For example: having its nails trimmed.

Wait until the dog is able to focus on the bucket, letting the dog adjust to whatever comfortable position suits it.

When the dog is focused on the bucket and able to hold focus for a few seconds, start moving your hand to the side of the dog without touching it. At this point, the dog can choose to continue looking at the bucket, in which case it receives a reward.

If the dog looks at your hand, it has communicated that it is uncomfortable. In this case, you need to stop; remember, this is the game of choice.

Once the dog re-engages with the bucket, the game begins again. This time, don't move your hand so quickly or so far. If the dog is able to maintain focus on the bucket, you can then reward it.

Keep doing this until the dog is happy to have its nails trimmed.

Important:

The game of choice will work only if you allow the dog to communicate that it wishes to either begin, break or stop the game.

If the dog looks away from the bucket, the game breaks/stops. When the dog re-engages with the bucket, you can continue with the game.

References

Domesticated Manners (2015). *"Teaching with Head & Heart"*. [online] Available at: http://www.domesticatedmanners.com/welcome/ [Accessed 21 Nov. 2015].

Patel, C. (2015). *The Bucket Game*. [online] Facebook.com. Available

https://www.facebook.com/thebucketgame/ [Accessed 21 Nov. 2015].

SCENARIO: BATHING & DRYING PROCESS

Setting the Scene

Breed & Coat Type: Jack Russell

Age: 5

Behaviour: Vocal

Health: Good

Bathing

Assess the dog and make sure the coat is in good condition and mat-free. Begin by introducing the shower hose, running the water to one side of the bath, away from the dog. Once the dog adjusts to the noise of the running water, slowly place the shower head close to the skin on the back of the dog. Move

> **HELPFUL TIP**
>
> A high pressure of water falling over a dog can overstimulate the dog. Intense washing can reinforce a dog's anxiety or fear.

the shower head in slow, circular motions over the dog's body, creating a waterfall effect. This technique can help a nervous dog more readily accept the contact of water and will prevent excitable behaviour from escalating.

Apply diluted shampoo through the sponge or scrunchie. Bathe the dog in circular motions, gradually moving towards the head. Using your fingers and hands with hypoallergenic shampoo, wash around the head and face area. Incorporate gentle ear work and/or Raccoon TTouch at the base of the ear or skull.

When rinsing, apply the same method that you did when wetting the dog, using a circular motion with the shower head. The Zebra TTouch can also be used to remove the shampoo whilst helping to calm a nervous dog.

> **HELPFUL TIP**
>
> **Rubbing the coat vigorously with the towel can escalate an already-aroused dog.**

Always keep your hand softly on the dog so that you maintain a connection. Avoid gripping too tightly.

Towel Drying

Once the coat is rinsed thoroughly, use a magic towel to take off excess water by gently kneading the coat, being mindful of sensitive areas. Avoid rubbing the coat.

> **HELPFUL TIP**
>
> **Don't use a circular motion to blast a long coat, as this can cause whip knots.**

> **HELPFUL TIP**
>
> **Using a hoodie when drying can help a noise-sensitive dog.**

Use of High-Velocity Dryer

Before switching on the dryer, place a Happy Hoodie on the dog's head if the dog is accepting of this. Then, at a low-level pressure, start blasting the dog from the rear, once again using slow, circular motions with the dryer nozzle. Increase the pressure of drying only if the dog is accepting.

Use of Finishing Dryer

An already-vocal dog can be helped by continued use of the hoodie whilst you finish drying the rest of the body. Start by letting the dog hear the dryer whilst on a low level. Then complete some touch work around the mouth area (for example, Baby Chimp TTouch). If the dog is accepting of this, continue with drying, taking care to watch for any hot spot areas that may escalate the vocalisation.

Nail Clipping See scenario pg 90

Touches Used Used		Equipment Used	Techniques
Ear Slides	(pg 46-47)	Sponge	TTouch
Raccoon	(pg 41)	Magic Towels	
Zebra	(pg 48-49)	Happy Hoodie	
Baby Chimp	(pg 42)		

SCENARIO: Dancing on the Table

Setting the Scene

Breed & Coat Type: Labradoodle

Age: 4 years old

Behaviour: Hates legs being touched

Health: Good

Styling Legs

Before trimming or clipping the legs, introduce a wrap or a Thundershirt and complete some gentle ear work. Then, with the back of the hand, very slowly stroke the body over the wrap and

> **HELPFUL TIP**
>
> **Thundershirts, like wraps, can be used in stressful situations.**

down the legs. Continue with the Zebra TTouch over the back and hindquarters, remembering to pause and give the dog a moment.

> **HELPFUL TIP**
>
> **Remember to pause and give the dog a chance to shake off, release tension, reorganise its body and process the information.**

Use a soft paint or makeup brush to stroke down each of the dog's legs, being mindful to not force acceptance. Once the dog is accepting of being touched, lift each leg without holding onto the foot, to encourage standing in balance.

Continue by completing gentle Python Lift TTouches on each leg, pausing after each one.

Let the dog hear and see the clippers before you put them on the legs. Once the dog is accepting, attempt to clip or scissor without overhandling. In some cases, let the dog keep its feet on the table so that it feels grounded.

> **HELPFUL TIP**
>
> **Getting the dog used to the sound of the clippers before putting them on the legs will "chunk" down the process step by step.**

If at any point the dog can't accept what is being done, go back to the point of the process during which the dog was comfortable. Start again, remembering to pause.

Touches Used		Equipment Used	Techniques Used
Ear Slides	(pg 46-47)	Paint/Makeup Brush	TTouch
Zebra	(pg 48-49)	Wrap/Thundershirt	
Python Lift	(pg 50-51)		

SCENARIO: PUPPY INTRODUCTION

Setting the Scene

Breed & Coat Type: Cockerpoo, first visit

Age: 4 months

Behaviour: Excitable

Health: Good

Welcome to the Grooming Room

> **HELPFUL TIP**
>
> **New learning experiences can create a positive outcome for a puppy or dog visiting the salon for the first time.**

To settle the puppy into the new environment, start by doing some free work for 5-10 minutes. Once the puppy has completed the free work, introduce the puppy to the grooming table to assess the coat. Make sure the puppy is mat- free prior to bathing. To do this, use a sheepskin mitt or soft paintbrush to gently stroke the puppy. Once the puppy accepts this initial process, introduce a brush or comb.

Every part of the grooming process must be taken step by step when introducing a puppy to the grooming environment.

Bathing

Begin by introducing the shower hose, running the water to one side of the bath, away from the puppy. Once

> **HELPFUL TIP**
>
> **Slow everything down and remember to pause.**

the puppy adjusts to the noise of the running water, slowly place the shower head close to the skin and move it in slow, circular motions over the puppy's body, creating a waterfall effect. This technique can prevent excitable puppy behaviour from escalating.

Apply diluted puppy shampoo through the sponge or scrunchie. Then, in circular motions, bathe the dog, gradually moving towards the head. Using your fingers and hands, wash around the head and face area. Incorporate gentle ear work and/or Raccoon TTouch at the base of the ear or skull.

When rinsing, apply the same method that you used when wetting the dog, using a circular motion with the shower head. The Zebra TTouch can also be used to help remove the shampoo whilst helping to calm an excitable puppy.

Always keep your hand softly on the puppy so that you maintain a connection. Avoid gripping too tightly.

Towel Drying

Once the coat is rinsed thoroughly, use a magic towel to remove excess water by gently kneading the coat, being mindful of sensitive areas. Avoid rubbing the coat.

> **HELPFUL TIP**
>
> "Chunk" the process into small steps so the puppy doesn't get overwhelmed.

Use of High-Velocity Dryer

Before switching on the dryer, place a Happy Hoodie on the puppy's head if the dog is accepting of this and wrap the puppy in a magic towel. Then, on a very low-level pressure, let the puppy hear the noise of the dryer. Start blasting the puppy from the rear over the top of the towel, once again using slow, circular motions with the dryer nozzle. If for any reason the puppy cannot cope with the blasting, stop, pause and complete some gentle ear work. If necessary, move on to the finishing dryer.

Use of Finishing Dryer

Start by letting the puppy hear the dryer whilst it is on a low level. Complete gentle hair slides. If the dog is accepting of this, continue to dry, taking care with the pressure of the brush or comb. If at any

> **HELPFUL TIP**
>
> **When applying TTouch, use a soft mitt if the puppy or dog is touch-sensitive.**

point the puppy's behaviour escalates, pause and give it a moment.

Once the puppy is dried and combed through, a second session of free work is beneficial, as it provides time for the puppy to process each stage. It also builds trust and confidence.

Introducing Clippers

A puppy introduction would not normally include clipping. However, it's important to get a new puppy used to the sounds of the

> **HELPFUL TIP**
>
> **It is important to build trust on the "first date" with a puppy or new dog.**

grooming environment. To do this, start by turning on the clippers away from the puppy so that the sound can be heard. Then complete Jelly Fish TTouch over the body. This combination will prepare a puppy for the contact of clipping at a future date.

Nail Clipping	see scenario pg 90	
Trimming Eyes	see scenario pg 88	

Touches Used Used		**Equipment Used**	**Techniques Used**
Ear Slides	(pg 46-47)	Sponge	TTouch
Raccoon	(pg 41)	Magic Towels	Free work
Zebra	(pg 48-49)	Happy Hoodie	
Jelly Fish	(pg 51)	Paint Brush	
Hair Slides	(pg 51-52)	Soft Mitt	

SCENARIO: Trimming Eyes

Setting the Scene

Breed & Coat Type: Shih Tzu, eye trim

Age: 3 years old

Behaviour: Reactive

Health: Good

Welcome to the Grooming Room

To settle a reactive or new dog into the grooming environment, start by doing some free work for 5-10 minutes. Once the dog has settled and has had the ability to choose to engage, a few simple TTouches (for example, the Zebra TTouch or ear work) may be incorporated. A body wrap may also be introduced before you attempt to put the dog on the table or in the bath.

> **HELPFUL TIP**
>
> **Sometimes it is better to trim the eyes in the bathing area rather than on the grooming table.**

Trimming Eyes

When you are trimming the eyes for the first time, start by introducing a soft makeup or small paint brush around the eye area. Slowly stroke down the sides of the face, between and over the head and eye area.

> **HELPFUL TIP**
>
> **Using different tools before you introduce scissors or clippers can help the dog accept a new process.**

Alternate between the brush and the scissors

without trimming the eyes, allowing the dog to accept the sensation of something close to its face and eyes. Continue with the Raccoon TTouch at the base of the skull, working over the ears and completing ear slides.

At all times, be mindful of speed and give the dog a chance to process by stopping and pausing. When the dog is accepting, trim the eyes.

If at any point the dog can't accept the scissors, revert to the brush and start the process again, remembering to pause.

Reference to Bella's Journey from Fear to Trust: https://www.youtube.com/watch?v=0NAEpqrjYns

Touches Used Used		Equipment Used	Techniques
Ear Slides	(pg 46-47)	Paint Brush	TTouch
Zebra	(pg 48-49)	Wrap	Free Work
Raccoon	(pg 41)		

SCENARIO: Trimming Nails

Setting the Scene

Breed & Coat Type: Cocker Spaniel, nail trim

Age: 5 years old

Behaviour: Hates feet being touched

Health: Good

Trimming Nails

Before trimming the nails or handling the feet, introduce a wrap and complete some gentle ear work. Then, with the nail

> **HELPFUL TIP**
>
> **If the dog can't cope with the nails clippers in sight, move them.**

clippers in sight, attempt the Raccoon TTouch on the toes, if possible while the dog is grounded on the table. If the dog doesn't like being handled around the feet, try some TTouch Air Circles with a small, soft makeup or paint brush.

> **HELPFUL TIP**
>
> **If the dog still doesn't like being handled, try some free work before moving back to the grooming table.**

When handling the feet and doing nails, be mindful to "contain" rather than restrain. If the dog resists being held, continue holding the paw in a non-threatening manner and move with the dog. This way, the dog has freedom of choice to move while you remain connected in a safe way. Pulling the dog's leg will only cause opposition reflex, with the dog pulling away and starting a "tug of war".

Whilst containing (and once the dog is accepting of being held), using the back of the hand to gently stroke down the legs to help the dog settle. Complete some gentle Raccoon TTouches over the feet and toes. If the dog can't cope with human contact, use a soft makeup brush or paintbrush to complete the TTouches. Alternate between the brush and using your fingers without trimming the nails at this point. Allow the dog to accept something close to the feet and toes.

HELPFUL TIP

Sometimes the sight or noise of the nail clippers is too much. Build the process step by step, helping to gain trust.

At all times be mindful of speed; give the dog a chance to process by stopping and pausing. Once the dog is accepting, attempt to cut the nails without overhandling. In some cases, cutting the nails can be achieved while the dog keeps its feet on the table so that it feels grounded.

If at any point the dog can't accept what is being done, return to the point of the process during which the dog was comfortable. Start again, remembering to pause. Remember, cutting one nail is one step closer to finishing; give the dog time.

Touches Used Used		Equipment Used	Techniques
Ear Slides	(pg 46-47)	Paint/Makeup Brush	TTouch
Air Circles	(pg 53)	Wrap	Free Work
Raccoon	(pg 41)		Contain Vs Restrain

Charles, Cocker Spaniel Success Story

Charles has a heart murmur and suffers from severe separation anxiety. When I first met Charles, I was told that other groomers had struggled to groom him due to his fear and because he couldn't have sedation. They said they couldn't complete his groom due to the risk of injury to themselves or out of a desire to avoid stressing him out even more.

Today we have managed to wash, dry and clip Charles. He even fell asleep whilst being dried. This is all because Mel and I put our TTouch skills into practice. We used a combination of TTouch bodywork techniques to help release tension and reduce stress. Each time Charles visits us, he develops more self-confidence and self-control.

By: Sarah Balmer –Trendy Pooches Bebington

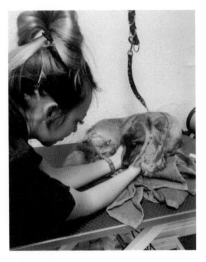

It is important to connect with the dog and begin building a bond with him.

Remember to PAUSE for a moment, giving the dog a chance to adjust and process what we are doing.

While doing pads or nails, we contain the paw rather than restrain. This gives him freedom and choice to move if he wants.

Bella, Shih Tzu Success Story

I'm sure this story will resonate with many groomers. Bella was four years old when she first visited my grooming salon. Her owners came to me because Bella was a very reactive little Shih Tzu. She had visited other groomers in the area with little success. In fact, no one could get close to her, let alone groom her.

Bella's story can be seen on YouTube – Bella's Journey from Fear to Trust: https://www.youtube.com/watch?v=0NAEpqrjYns

In the video, you will see how Bella's posture and behaviour changed significantly after a very short period of time. By applying a few simple TTouch Techniques, I helped to calm Bella. She was able to release the built-up tension she was carrying, I helped to build trust and a connection with her. As a result, I was able to groom her without using fear or force, all thanks to the magic of **TTOUCH**.

About the Authors

Glynis Stewart has been a dog groomer for over 10 years. She has successfully franchised her company, Trendy Pooches Dog Grooming, and is proud to see her brand grow into eight successful grooming salons – five of them offering a Self-Serve Dog Wash facility. After becoming a qualified TTouch Practitioner (P2), she decided to open a grooming training academy to incorporate Tellington TTouch® in all grooming courses. Alongside her very dear friend Dawn, she has spent the past six years travelling throughout the UK, teaching workshops and speaking at various grooming events/colleges. She lives in Wirral with her husband John and her four dogs, Tilly, Ruby, Alfie and Oscar. She has two daughters, Nicola and Sarah (who also run their own grooming salons), and a son, Paul.

Glynis is forever grateful for the help, support and guidance that her family have given her, especially her husband John and father Bob Evans.

Dawn Harkin has over 10 years of dog grooming experience. She lives in Lancashire and runs a successful dog grooming training academy, grooming spa, self-serve facility and retail shop.

She is a qualified Groomer Tellington TTouch® Practitioner (P2) and specialises in handling dogs in the grooming environment. She teaches workshops around the UK at colleges and other grooming centres. Alongside her dear friend and colleague Glynis, she has demonstrated her skills at various dog grooming events throughout the country.

Dawn currently shares her home with two of the stars of this book, Nellie and Zac, who are her faithful friends and companions, and the other star, Herman, who watches over from the Rainbow Bridge.

FINAL WORD

This book was born out of a desire to make a difference to every groomer and the dogs that pass through our salons on a daily basis. As we know, grooming can be a very challenging but rewarding career. We hope the tips and techniques in this book will inspire you to be the best handler you can be in circumstances that are sometimes very demanding.

Anything that we can use in our daily working routines to enrich the grooming process and environment for both groomer and the dogs in our care has to be a bonus.

So, keep trying. During your first attempt, it might feel different, or you might be unsure about whether the techniques will work. However, we can promise you one thing: You will see results and the benefits will far outweigh the time and effort it takes to apply the techniques.

Wishing you the best of luck. Stand back and be amazed.

Dawn & Glyn

Quick Reference Guide

This checklist is a quick reference to help you find a solution to typical grooming challenges:

ISSUE	POTENTIAL SOLUTION
Concern with water	Zebra, Ear TTouches, circular touches with sponge or scrunchie
Fear of dryer	Jelly Fish TTouch, Zebra, Mouth TTouch, Happy Hoodie, body wrap
Concern with clippers	Jelly Fish, TTouch, body wrap
Fear of scissors between eyes	Ear TTouches, Raccoon TTouch, makeup brush
Anxious about nail clipping	Python TTouches, air circles, Raccoon TTouch, makeup brush, Sheepskin mitt
Fear of trimming feet and pads	Python TTouch, Raccoon TTouch, makeup brush
Clipping legs	Python TTouch, Jelly Fish

Anxious with ear plucking	Ear TTouch, hair slides, body wrap
Concern with brushing	Hair slides, TTouches with sheepskin mitt, makeup brush
Hyperactivity	Clouded Leopard TTouch, Mouth TTouch, Ear TTouch, free work
Vocalisation	Free work, body wrap or face wrap, hair scrunchie, Tail TTouch
Urinating due to stress or excitement	Ear TTouch, Zebra TTouch
Shyness	Ear TTouch, Lying Leopard TTouch, Tail TTouch
Separation anxiety	Lying Leopard TTouch, Ear TTouch, body wrap, free work
Fear of travel	Ear TTouch, body wrap or Thundershirt
Chewing	Mouth TTouch, hair scrunchie
Arthritis	Python TTouch, Raccoon TTouch, Ear TTouch, body wrap

Fearful of human contact	Llama TTouch, sponge, sheepskin mitt, free work
Elderly dogs with stiff joints	Zebra TTouch
Sensitivity around head or mouth	Chimp TTouch, Raccoon TTouch
Fear of grooming environment	Free work, body wrap or Thundershirt, Ear TTouch
Dancing on the table	Ear TTouch, Zebra TTouch, Python TTouch, Thundershirt or body wrap

Useful Addresses & Acknowledgements

Dawn Harkin

Mutz Cutz Grooming Academy
97 Station Rd
Bamber Bridge
Lancashire, PR5 6QS
www.mutz-cutz.co.uk
email: mutzcutzuk@gmail.com

Glynis Stewart

Trendy Pooches Grooming Academy
Market House
9 Oakenholt Road,
Moreton
Wirral CH46 8TP
0151 678 2041
www.academy@trendypooches.com
www.trendypooches.com
email: glynis@trendypooches.co.uk

Robyn Hood
TTouch Canada
5435 Rochdell Road
Vernon BC1VB 3E8

www.tteam-ttouch.ca
Linda Tellington Jones
TTouch USA
PO Box 3793
Santa Fe
New Mexico 87501
USA
www.ttouch.com

Sarah Fisher
TTouch UK
Tilley Farm,
Bath BA2 0AB
01761471 1182
www.ttouchteam.co.uk
email: sarahfisher@ttouchteam.co.uk

Acknowledgements

With thanks to:

Sarah Fisher, Robyn Hood, Linda Tellington Jones, Chirag Patel, Turid Rugaas, Dr Daniela Zurr DVM and Colin Taylor, who was the first to invite us to speak at Master Groom about TTouch. We also thank Tony Cruse for his help and recommendations about publishing. A special thanks to our caring professional team members who support our ethos, "welfur before furcut", and all the canine volunteers that helped us produce this book.

Printed in Great Britain
by Amazon